Deadly History

THE MAYA

FEARSOME FIGHTERS AND SCARY SACRIFICE

CHERITON CHILDREN'S BOOKS

Picture credits: Cover: Shutterstock/Leon Rafael (foreground), Shutterstock/Millionstock (background); Inside: p1: Shutterstock/Cezary Wojtkowski; p4: Shutterstock/Aleksandr Medvedkov; p5: Shutterstock/Terra Adentro; p6: Shutterstock/Mardoz; p7: Shutterstock/Nikidel; p8: Shutterstock/Patryk Kosmider; p9: Shutterstock/Leon Rafael; p10: Wikimedia Commons/Michel Wal; p11: Shutterstock/Oleg Elkov; p12: Wikimedia Commons/De Young Museum/Daderot; p13: Shutterstock/Oleg Elkov; p14: Wikimedia Commons/Futons of Rock; p15: Wikimedia Commons/New Orleans Museum of Art/Infrogmation of New Orleans; p16: Shutterstock/Leon Rafael; p17: Wikimedia Commons/AlejandroLinaresGarcia; p18: Wikimedia Commons/Wmpearl; p19: Shutterstock/Wasanajai; p20: Wikimedia Commons/FA2010; p21: Wikimedia Commons/HJPD; p22: Shutterstock/Tetris Awakening; p23: Wikimedia Commons/Akubra; p24: Shutterstock/AlexAranda; p25: Shutterstock/David Pegzlz; p26: Shutterstock/Cezary Wojtkowski; p27: Shutterstock/Pixel-Shot; p28: Shutterstock/Vladimir Korostyshevskiy; p29: Shutterstock/AAR Studio; p30: Shutterstock/Cezary Wojtkowski; p31: Shutterstock/Vladimir Korostyshevskiy; p32: Wikimedia Commons/Peter Andersen; p33: Shutterstock/Frontpage; p34: Shutterstock/AB Photographie; p35: Wikimedia Commons/Walters Art Museum; p36: Shutterstock/Dowraik; p37: Wikimedia Commons/Dorieo; p38: Wikimedia Commons/David at MARI; p39: Wikimedia Commons/Salvador Alc; p40: Shutterstock/Ernest2099; p41: Shutterstock/Vlad G; p42: Wikimedia Commons/Wolfgang Sauber; p43: Shutterstock/Sanit Fuangnakhon; p44: Shutterstock/TLF Images; p45: Shutterstock/Oleg Elkov.

Printed in China

Please visit our website,
www.cheritonchildrensbooks.com
to see more of our high-quality books.

CONTENTS

CHAPTER 1

BUILT ON FEAR

The Maya were a powerful people who lived in Central America from 300 to 900 CE. Mayan ruins are evidence that their **civilization** was very advanced. However, they also show that it was built on blood and fear.

The Mayan city of Chichén Itzá shows that the Maya created an impressive civilization.

Dark and Deadly!

The most feared animal in the Mayan world was the jaguar, the largest and most powerful cat in the Americas. This **predator** has razor-sharp claws and deadly fangs.

Forests of Danger

The **rain forests** in which most Maya lived were full of dangers. There were deadly biting insects, fierce pumas, sharp-toothed crocodiles, and **venomous** snakes. The Maya also lived in fear of **evil spirits**, from which only their powerful gods could protect them.

Blood Worship

The Maya worshiped more than 150 different gods, most of which had both a good and evil side. The Maya believed that to keep safe and successful, it was necessary to offer their gods **sacrifices** of animal and human blood. They carried out these sacrifices at the top of **temples**.

It must have been amazing to discover the Mayan ruins in the rain forest.

Sinister Cities

The first Maya were farmers who lived in small villages and towns. Gradually, power-hungry kings took control of whole areas. They ruled all the settlements around their large city strictly, and sometimes unfairly.

Built on Blood

The Maya built some cities and took over others left by previous ancient peoples. These cities were built on blood. For example, beneath a temple in Teotihuacán lay the bodies of headless animals and people sacrificed to make each layer of the pyramid **sacred** as it was built.

Sacrifice at the Center

The king's palace and the temples where sacrifices were carried out lay in the center of Mayan cities. The palaces were several stories high, with courtyards, gardens, and towers. However, ordinary Mayan families lived in windowless houses that had just one room, built on a platform of dirt to keep the rains from **flooding** them.

Headless skeletons and skulls separated from their bodies have been found at many Mayan sites.

Dark and Deadly!

The walls of Mayan cities were covered in carvings of gods and strange **mythical** creatures. These scary-looking creations kept ordinary people living in fear of the powerful gods that ruled their lives.

The main street through Teotihuacán was named the Avenue of the Dead.

Bloody Battles

Mayan kings regularly led their armies on bloodthirsty attacks against other cities. Warriors fought vicious battles day after day, until one side finally won.

Savage Battles

The savage battles were fought so one city could win more land from another city, and to claim valuable treasures or goods. Kings also attacked other cities to capture enemies to use as **slaves** and for sacrifices. The **priests** who performed the sacrifices often told warriors when captives for sacrifice were needed.

Mayan warriors were armed with deadly weapons, and their appearance was designed to terrify their enemies.

The Losers Pay

Warriors fought battles only during the day. A battle continued until the leader of one army was hurt or killed. Then the losers had to pay a **tribute** to the winners. The tribute could include goods, salt, textiles, gold, silver, copper, and even people.

Dark and Deadly!

Murderous Mayan warriors loved nothing more than capturing high-ranking enemies. These prisoners were taken home, where they were often murdered.

Mayan kings were constantly fighting vicious and bloodthirsty battles against each other.

CHAPTER 2

SCARY DRESSERS

The Mayan kings were all-powerful. The royals and **nobles** took every chance they had to show off their wealth. They wore some **macabre** outfits to demonstrate to people how powerful and important they were.

Amazing Headdresses

Royals and nobles also wore headdresses made from hundreds of beautiful and valuable feathers plucked from rare birds, which they kept in cages. Some headdresses were taller than the people who wore them!

WHY DO YOU THINK IT WAS IMPORTANT FOR MAYAN KINGS TO SHOW OFF THEIR WEALTH AND POWER?

Mayan pots and walls often show kings and wealthy people wearing rich clothing and headdresses.

Important people, such as nobles and priests, wore impressive headdresses.

Dark and Deadly!

Royals and nobles were the only people allowed to wear the long, bright-green tail feathers of the quetzal bird in their hair or headdresses. If an ordinary Maya wore feathers, their punishment could be death.

Signs of Power

Kings often wore skins of jaguars or other dangerous animals as a **symbol** of their power. Jaguars could sneak up on victims silently or leap onto them suddenly from trees. They were seen as magical and terrifying, so kings thought people would fear them if they wore jaguar skins.

Scary Bodies

Mayan kings and nobles not only wore macabre costumes, but they also modified, or changed, the way they looked. The Maya believed that the more important a person was, the more extreme their body modifications should be.

Talking to the Gods

The Maya thought that body modifications not only looked good, but were also a way to communicate with their gods. They believed their suffering and bleeding during these treatments were an exchange for the food, rain, and life that the gods gave to them.

Terrifying Teeth

Sometimes, kings, priests, and nobles modified their teeth, too. They drilled holes into their teeth and then put pieces of precious stones such as jade, **obsidian**, or turquoise into the holes.

This model shows a warrior, with facial scars. The scars were made by cutting patterns into the skin.

Dark and Deadly!

When the Maya went to war, warriors had their teeth filed into sharp points. This was not only a way to ask the gods for victory in war, but it also made the warriors look more ferocious to help them scare their enemies.

Body paint and piercings made the Maya look even fiercer to enemies.

Faces of Fear

The Maya's fear of their gods led them to take some desperate measures. They did all they could to please their gods, even changing the shape of their heads.

Changing Children

Some noble families tried to make their children look like the god of maize, who had a long, stretched head. They strapped boards to the front and back of a baby's head so that it would grow longer and thinner.

A mirror-bearer, like this model of one, held up a mirror for the ruler to look at his reflection. A mirror was often aimed at a ruler while he was on his throne.

WHY DO YOU THINK THE MAYA WERE PREPARED TO SUFFER IN ORDER TO PLEASE THEIR GODS?

Cross-Eyed Pleasers

Some mothers hung a bead from the hair on their child's forehead so that it dangled permanently in front of their nose. This was meant to make the child cross-eyed. Parents did this to please and honor the sun god, who was shown as cross-eyed.

The Maya believed that long and thin heads, such as the one shown in this statue, were impressive.

Dark and Deadly!

The Maya did not just use obsidian mirrors to check their appearance. Men looked into a mirror to show how brave they were. The Maya believed that evil creatures could reach through an obsidian mirror and drag them down into the **underworld**.

CHAPTER 3

BRUTAL BATTLES

Mayan warriors prepared for battle by making themselves look as fierce and terrifying as possible. They often used jaguar teeth and claws to decorate their bodies, shields, and spears.

Frightened Fighters

Some Mayan warriors wore scary masks in battle. They were used for protection, because the wearers believed the masks gave them a god-like power. The masks were also used to scare enemies—making them terrified even before any fighting began.

Mayan warriors wore body paint and parts of deadly animals to terrify their enemies.

Deadly Killers

Warriors often had paintings or tattoos of animals such as snakes, eagles, or jaguars on their face and body. These were some of the most dangerous animals in the Mayan world. The tattoos were created by piercing the skin with needles. Warriors wore images of these fearsome animals to show how important they were.

Dark and Deadly!

Some Mayan warriors are said to have worn a necklace of shrunken heads of previous enemies they had killed to warn other opponents just how dangerous they were.

The Maya wore masks like this one into battle.

Weapons for War

Mayan warriors charged at their enemies using a variety of vicious and deadly weapons. They also used **tear gas** and bombs to attack them.

Fighting Tools

Mayan warriors had stone weapons as well as weapons made of wood and shells. They fought with spears, slings, clubs, axes, and knives. They also carved obsidian rock into razor-sharp spear tips. They topped the arrows they shot from their bows with jagged fish teeth.

Tear Gas Attack

The Maya also invented a type of tear gas. They burned large amounts of hot chilis to create a horrible smoke, which they blew toward the enemy. The thick, fiery smoke stung opponents' eyes and skin. While the enemies struggled to breathe and see, the Mayan warriors attacked.

Shields with fierce faces carved into them were designed to terrify.

Dark and Deadly!

The Maya made grenades using gourds, which are large fruits with a hard skin. They hollowed out the shell of the gourds and filled them with wasps and bees. Then they threw these grenades at their enemies.

The hole at the top of the gourd was filled with grass to keep the insects from escaping.

WHAT DO YOU THINK THE MAYA'S INVENTIVE WARFARE TELLS US ABOUT THEM?

Suffering Slaves

When Mayan warriors won a battle, they brought back captured enemies. Some of these prisoners of war became slaves. They were forced to work for the king, nobles, priests, and farmers for free.

Horrible Jobs

Slaves did all the worst jobs. They cleared routes through dangerous jungles and insect-infested swamps. Traders could then travel along these routes to buy and sell goods such as gold and jaguar skins. The slaves also had to carry these heavy goods long distances in baskets on their backs.

This carving shows captives being presented to a ruler to become his slaves.

Backbreaking Work

Slaves were forced to work on enormous building projects such as temples and palaces. They carried stone and other materials on their backs or rolled them on logs from a **quarry** to the building site. Then they hacked away at the stone for many hours in the heat to make the buildings.

The Maya made their slaves carve important symbols into stone. Some carvings, like this one, showed the name of a Mayan ruler. His name was Great Jaguar Paw.

Dark and Deadly!

Some Maya became slaves as a form of punishment if they committed certain crimes or failed to pay what they owed. The poorest families sometimes sold a relative into slavery to make money.

CHAPTER 4

BLOODY GIFTS

The Maya believed that their gods controlled everything on Earth. If something bad happened, such as a violent storm, they thought the gods were angry with them. For the Maya, **offerings** of blood were the only way to keep the gods happy.

Dark and Deadly!

Some animals were sacrificed and their blood used as offerings to the gods. Animals such as turkeys, dogs, squirrels, lizards, and crocodiles were sacrificed in great numbers.

The Maya performed many ceremonies for their gods to try and please them.

Blood-Hungry Gods

Bloodletting was the most common way that the Maya fed their ever-hungry gods with blood. They would cut themselves until they bled. Sometimes, a king used a knife or the sharp spine of a stingray to cut his skin and let the blood drop into a bowl.

Help from the Gods

Bloodletting was also a way to speak to the gods in order to ask for their help. Sometimes, the blood released from the painful wound was used to soak paper. Then, the paper was burned to send the blood and the people's prayers to the gods.

This carved panel shows a bloodletting **ritual** in which a Mayan queen pulls a spiked rope through her tongue.

Scary Sacrifices

The most important blood offerings came from human sacrifices. Human sacrifices took place in large numbers to celebrate a great victory in battle. Sometimes, many slaves were sacrificed at once to stop a terrible disaster, such as a severe **drought** or flood.

Horrible Deaths

Humans who were sacrificed were killed with a sharp, sacrificial knife. Others might be killed by an arrow to their heart, having their head cut off, or being thrown off the side of a high cliff. Some unfortunate victims died slowly as their skin was stripped from their body.

Dark and Deadly!

Some sacrificial knives were made from obsidian. Obsidian could be made into sharper blades than steel.

Sinkhole Sacrifices

Sacrifices to Chac, the Mayan god of rain, were made by throwing victims into sinkholes. These are deep wells created when underground streams made cave roofs collapse. The Maya believed that these holes were direct routes to some of their gods.

The skulls of sacrificial victims have been found at the bottom of sinkholes such as this one.

WHY DO YOU THINK THE MAYA BELIEVED SINKHOLES WERE SPECIAL PLACES?

Glassy obsidian rock forms from volcanic lava as it cools. The rock is sharpened into a blade.

Bloody Ball Games

Even Mayan ball games involved death and offerings of blood! Some games reenacted a battle between gods of the day and night, or good and evil.

The Rules

Mayan ball games were played on a large court with two sloping walls opposite one another. Two teams passed a large ball to each other using only their knees, elbows, or hips. A point was scored by getting the ball through a stone ring set high on the court walls.

It was difficult to bounce a ball through stone hoops on the high walls without using hands.

The leader from the losing team, usually an important enemy ruler, was sacrificed to the gods.

Winners and Losers

Warriors often played ball games against prisoners of war they had captured. The winners of the game were treated as heroes and given a feast. The losing players lost more than the game—they were killed.

After the leader of the losing team was sacrificed, a new ball was made with his skull!

CHAPTER 5

TEMPLES OF TERROR

Mayan priests held gruesome ceremonies at the pyramids. These temples of terror were built incredibly high up and sacrifices were carried out at the very top of them.

Climbing to Die

Huge crowds of people gathered at the base of the temple for the festivals held to honor Mayan gods. After days of ceremonies, music, feasting, and dancing, the priests painted blue the person that they intended to sacrifice. Then they forced them to climb the pyramid.

The Maya designed their temples to be terrifying and impressive, like their warriors.

Closer to the Gods

The pyramids used for ceremonies had two to four sets of steep staircases all the way to the top. As priests climbed up the high steps, they left Earth behind and moved toward the sky. They believed that this brought them and their sinister sacrifices closer to the gods.

Mayan priests who climbed to the top of a pyramid to make sacrifices were very important, powerful people.

Dark and Deadly!

A second type of pyramid had steps that were almost too steep to climb. This type of temple was sacred and not meant to be touched. The pyramid often had secret tunnels, traps, and doorways that led to dead ends.

Platforms of Fear

Sacrifices were made at special ceremonies on the large, flat platforms at the top of the high pyramids. The priests wore fierce-looking costumes and the huge crowds of people below watched them in awe and fear.

Held Down to Die

The priest led the victim to a stone **altar** on the temple platform. Helpers held down the victim while the priest quickly cut open their chest with a ceremonial knife. The priest removed the victim's heart while it was still beating.

Dark and Deadly!

Priests wore scary masks and costumes at religious ceremonies. They wanted to strike fear into the hearts of ordinary people and appear as powerful and terrifying as the gods themselves.

The Maya believed that sacrifices held on temple platforms fed the gods and made sure the world would survive.

Skinned Sacrifices

The victim's blood was then smeared onto an image of the god. The victim's body was often hurled down the temple steps where assistant priests removed its skin. A high priest then often wore the skin of the victim and performed a ritual dance in it.

Important warriors captured in battle by powerful Mayan fighters were valuable sacrifices.

Racks of Skulls

The skulls of people who had been sacrificed were often placed on display on racks outside the temples, along with stone carvings that showed the skull racks.

Skinning the Skull

After a sacrifice, priests used their sharp obsidian knives to cut away the skin and muscles from a murdered victim, leaving only the skull. Then, they carved large holes in the sides of the skull so a thick wooden post could be pushed through the skull.

Put on Display

Rows of skulls were also displayed on huge racks near a ball court. The losers of ball games were often beheaded and had their skulls placed on the skull rack. Sometimes, skulls were piled one on top of another on tall posts.

WHAT EFFECT MAY THE SKULL RACKS NEAR A BALL COURT HAVE HAD ON PEOPLE ABOUT TO PLAY THE GAME?

This is a stone carving of a skull rack. It must have been a terrifying sight for people.

Dark and Deadly!

Skull racks were built to show off how many enemies had been killed in a war, to frighten enemies, and to also celebrate and remember those killed in sacrifice to the gods.

This is the skeleton of a Mayan sacrifice victim. The Maya were convinced that people who were sacrificed went to heaven.

DEADLY AFTER DEATH

The Maya believed in three worlds: an upper world of peace and happiness in heaven, the middle world of Earth, and a dark and horrible underworld. This was where Maya went in their **afterlife**, once they died.

Death and Danger

The Maya thought the underworld had nine layers, each with an evil god. The underworld was ruled by the most feared Maya god of all, the Lord of Death. The evil gods of the underworld used **demons** and other horrifying creatures to torment people.

The Maya named the underworld Xibalba, which means "the place of fright." One of the dangers they faced there were terrifying jaguars.

Terrifying Tests

The cruel demons and monsters of the underworld forced dead Maya to undergo terrifying tests of courage and skill. Maya who survived this dangerous place and its demons would be allowed to go to heaven forever more.

Dark and Deadly!

The macabre challenges the Maya faced in the underworld included a river of poisonous scorpions, and a game played with balls of turning blades.

The demons of the underworld could cause pain, disease, starvation, and even transform skeletons.

35

Living with the Dead

When most ordinary Maya died, they were wrapped in a simple cotton cloth and buried beneath the floors of their house. This meant that for most Maya, the house that they lived in was both a family home and a **tomb**.

The Color of Death

Before burial, relatives would paint the body with a red mineral called cinnabar. Red was the color of death and rebirth for the Maya, so they often covered graves with cinnabar, too.

Useful and important items such as pots and dishes were often buried with dead bodies.

Dark and Deadly!

Before it was buried, maize was placed in the mouth of a dead person. The Maya believed this food would nourish the dead on their journey through the dark and dangerous underworld.

Still Needed

Families also buried a dead person's most important belongings alongside the body. They believed that the dead person would be able to have and use these things in the afterlife.

Some Maya were burned and their ashes put in urns like this one before burial.

Pleasing the Dead

Burying dead relatives under a house may sound creepy, but it gave the Maya great comfort. They believed that burying their relatives beneath homes allowed the **ancestors** to watch over them and help keep them safe.

Don't Forget

The Maya had many traditions to remember relatives who died. They regularly put offerings near where their loved ones were buried. They usually left these offerings several times a year, during feasts and on festival days.

This carving shows the god Itzamna on the right, whom the Maya believed could bring the dead back to life.

The Maya usually left food and objects related to the dead relative's former life as offerings at their grave site.

Never Forgotten

When a house became damaged, Mayan families sometimes abandoned it. When it left, the family still treated the house with the same respect as they would a tomb. The family would return to the house to give offerings to the dead there.

Dark and Deadly!

The Maya feared that if they did not please the gods, they would release demons from the underworld. Then the demons would attack and destroy them. By worshiping the ancestors, they hoped they would prevent this.

Terrible Tombs

While ordinary people were buried under houses, Mayan kings were laid to rest in special tombs, often under their palaces or in giant pyramids. These tombs held some dark secrets.

Filled with Treasure

Mayan kings were often buried in small rooms inside the pyramid. Their tombs were beautifully decorated and filled with treasures, such as pendants made from gold and rare gemstones. These were for the king to use in the afterlife.

This king was buried with important possessions.

Dark and Deadly!

Regular offerings were left to dead kings at the royal tombs. It is also believed that living rulers used bloodletting rituals to contact specific ancestors from their royal family to ask them for help.

For the Maya, symbolism and ritual were very important parts of life and death.

Sacrificed Slaves

When a king died, he did not travel to the afterlife alone. Unfortunate members of the royal family or court officials were often sacrificed so they could accompany him. Slaves were also killed when their owners died, so that they could continue their service after death.

Masks of Death

The Maya believed that when a mighty and powerful king died, he would become a god. That is why kings were buried with their faces covered by spooky-looking death masks.

Like a King

Death masks were often made to look like a king when he was alive. They were usually made from jade, a rare green stone. This was the most sacred and precious of all materials in the Mayan world.

This is the jade burial mask of Pakal the Great, king of the city of Palenque, who ruled from the age of 12 to 80.

Another God

The Maya believed that an expensive and elaborate death mask would prove to the gods that the dead person was an important king when he arrived in the underworld. The mask would help the gods of the underworld recognize him and treat him as another god.

Dark and Deadly!

When a king or official died, priests pried open his mouth and put a jade bead inside. The Maya believed that the jade would help the **corpse** breathe again and come back from the dead.

For the Maya, jade was a symbol of eternal life.

DEATH OF THE MAYA

The murderous Maya ruled over their bloodthirsty civilization for about 600 years. Then their cities were abandoned and the Maya were gone.

Deadly Killers

Some experts think that a deadly disease wiped out most of the Maya. It also seems likely that many people in Mayan cities were killed in violent attacks from other cities or by **invaders** from other lands.

The amazing **monuments** left behind by the Maya remind us of their incredible civilization.

Dark and Deadly!

Some scientists say that a terrible drought struck around the time the Maya disappeared. With no rain, plants did not grow and there was nothing to drink. Perhaps the Maya slowly starved to death.

Ending Their World

The Maya may have brought about their own end by their farming methods. They burned down trees to clear land for farming. Over time, this damaged the soil and made it useless for growing **crops**. In the end, perhaps many Maya fled the region to find new land that they could farm and live on.

The Maya are sometimes remembered today through the reenactment of their mysterious and awe-inspiring culture.

GLOSSARY

afterlife life after death. Some people believe that after we die we go to live in another world

altar a table or platform on which religious rituals are carried out

ancestors relatives who have died

civilization a settled community in which people live together and use systems such as writing to communicate

corpse a dead body

crops plants grown for food

demons evil spirits or devils

drought a period of time with little or no rainfall

evil spirits dangerous supernatural beings

flooding when water covers an area of land that is usually dry

invaders people, armies, or countries that use force to enter and take control of another country

macabre gruesome

monuments statues, buildings, or other structures made to remember events, times, or people

mythical describes something from a traditional, well-known, but made-up story

nobles people in the highest class in certain societies

obsidian a hard, dark, glass-like volcanic rock

offerings things that people give as part of a religious ceremony or ritual

predator an animal that kills and eats other animals

priests religious leaders

quarry an open mine

rain forests thick forests of tall trees found in wet areas

ritual a ceremony performed for religious reasons

sacred important to a religion

sacrifices things killed to honor a god or gods

slaves people who are owned by other people and must obey them

symbol an image that represents something else

tear gas a gas that burns the eyes and makes them water

temples buildings that people visit to worship their god or gods

tomb a building where dead people are laid to rest

tribute a gift of food or other items paid by people to their ruler

underworld the mythical world of the dead

venomous poisonous

FIND OUT MORE

Books

Spilsbury, Louise. *Forensic Investigations of the Maya* (Forensic Footprints of the Ancient Worlds). Crabtree Publishing Company, 2018.

Tyler, Madeline. *The Ancient Maya* (Unlocking Ancient Civilizations). Kidhaven, 2019.

Williams, Brian. *Maya, Incas, and Aztecs* (DK Findout!). DK Children, 2018.

Websites

This website has a lot of pictures, facts, and other information about the Maya:
http://mexicolore.co.uk/maya

Find out the top 10 Mayan secrets at:
www.nationalgeographic.com/travel/top-10/maya-secrets

Read theories about why the Maya disappeared at:
**http://science.nasa.gov/science-news/science-at-
nasa/2009/06oct_maya**

Publisher's note to educators and parents:
All the websites featured above have been carefully reviewed to ensure that they are suitable for students. However, many websites change often, and we cannot guarantee that a site's future contents will continue to meet our high standards of educational value. Please be advised that students should be closely monitored whenever they access the Internet.

INDEX

About the Authors

Sarah Eason and Louise Spilsbury have written many history books for children. Both love finding out about past people, and through writing this book have learned how deadly daily life really was for people who lived during the age of the merciless Maya.